WITNESS TO HISTORY

NEIL ARMSTRONG

in his own words

NASA ARMSTRONG

Gareth Stevens
PUBLISHING

By
Ryan
Nagelhout

Please visit our website, www.garethstevens.com. For a free color catalog of all our high-quality books, call toll free 1-800-542-2595 or fax 1-877-542-2596.

Library of Congress Cataloging-in-Publication Data

Nagelhout, Ryan, author.
 Neil Armstrong in his own words / Ryan Nagelhout.
    pages cm. — (Eyewitness to history)
 Includes bibliographical references and index.
 ISBN 978-1-4824-4078-2 (pbk.)
 ISBN 978-1-4824-4079-9 (6 pack)
 ISBN 978-1-4824-4080-5 (library binding)
 1. Armstrong, Neil, 1930-2012—Juvenile literature. 2. Project Apollo (U.S.)—History—Juvenile literature. 3. Astronauts—United States—Biography—Juvenile literature. 4. Space flight to the moon—History—Juvenile literature. I. Title. II. Series: Eyewitness to history (Gareth Stevens Publishing)
 TL789.85.A75N34 2016
 629.450092—dc23
 [B]

                                        2015034674

First Edition

Published in 2016 by
Gareth Stevens Publishing
111 East 14th Street, Suite 349
New York, NY 10003

Copyright © 2016 Gareth Stevens Publishing

Designer: Katelyn E. Reynolds
Editor: Therese Shea

Photo credits: Cover, pp. 1 (Neil Armstrong and background image), 10–11, 15, 17, 19, 23, 25 courtesy of NASA; cover, p. 1 (logo quill icon) Seamartini Graphics Media/Shutterstock.com; cover, p. 1 (logo stamp) YasnaTen/Shutterstock.com; cover, p. 1 (color grunge frame) DmitryPrudnichenko/Shutterstock.com; cover, pp. 1–32 (paper background) Nella/Shutterstock.com; cover, pp. 1–32 (decorative elements) Ozerina Anna/Shutterstock.com; pp. 1–32 (wood texture) Reinhold Leitner/Shutterstock.com; pp. 1–32 (open book background) Elena Schweitzer/Shutterstock.com; pp. 1–32 (bookmark) Robert Adrian Hillman/Shutterstock.com; p. 5 Hulton Archive/Getty Images; pp. 7, 21 NASA/Newsmakers; p. 9 Michael Hickey/Getty Images; p. 13 Jatkins/Wikipedia.org; p. 18 Keystone/Getty Images; p. 27 Stobkcuf/Wikipedia.org; p. 28 (signature) McSush/Wikipedia.org.

Printed in the United States of America

CPSIA compliance information: Batch #CW16GS: For further information contact Gareth Stevens, New York, New York at 1-800-542-2595.

CONTENTS

*Words in the glossary appear in **bold** type the first time they are used in the text.*

Not a HEARTBEAT Wasted

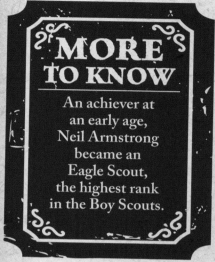

MORE TO KNOW

An achiever at an early age, Neil Armstrong became an Eagle Scout, the highest rank in the Boy Scouts.

Neil Alden Armstrong died on August 25, 2012. A few weeks later, he was buried at sea in the Atlantic Ocean. In 1969, it was a different ocean—the Pacific—where Armstrong and two other astronauts splashed down in the command **module** of the Apollo spacecraft, completing one of the most important missions in human history.

*"I believe that every human has a **finite** number of heartbeats,"* Armstrong once said. *"And I don't intend to waste any of mine."* In his 82 years on Earth—and the few days he spent off it—Neil Armstrong stayed true to those words. During those years, he was a navy pilot, an astronaut, a professor, and more. This remarkable man lived a remarkable life—which included uttering some famous words where no human had ever been before.

After his historic mission to space, Neil Armstrong became one of the most famous people on Earth. However, he tried to live a quiet life.

SPECIAL RECORDING: "SOUNDS OF THE SPACE AGE" (page 750)

VOL. 136, NO. 6 — DECEMBER 1969

NATIONAL GEOGRAPHIC

FIRST EXPLORERS ON THE MOON

THE INCREDIBLE STORY OF APOLLO 11 IN FIVE PARTS 735

YANKEE SAILS TURKEY'S HISTORY-HAUNTED COAST 798
IRVING AND ELECTA JOHNSON
JOSEPH SCHERSCHEL

INSIDE A HORNBILL'S WALLED-UP NEST 846
JOAN AND ALAN ROOT

CHARTRES: LOVELY LEGACY OF THE AGE OF FAITH 857
KENNETH MacLEISH
DEAN CONGER

"...in peace for all mankind"

OFFICIAL JOURNAL OF THE NATIONAL GEOGRAPHIC SOCIETY WASHIN

MORE THAN A MOON MAN

Armstrong is best known as the first man to step foot on the moon as the commander of the *Apollo 11* mission. He was often called a "reluctant" and "humble" hero because he shied away from the fame that mission brought. In 2005, Armstrong said, *"I guess we all like to be recognized not for one piece of fireworks, but for the ledger of our daily work."* He was proud of his other accomplishments, too.

FASCINATED
by Flight

THE "TIN GOOSE"

Armstrong's father encouraged Neil's interest in airplanes at an early age. Their first flight took place in a Ford Trimotor plane nicknamed the "Tin Goose." Neil and Stephen boarded the plane in Warren, Ohio. The two were thrilled by the flight. *"We were supposed to be at church, I think,"* Armstrong later said. *"But we sneaked off and later my mother caught us, just because of the guilty, and probably excited, looks on our faces."*

Neil Armstrong was born on his grandparents' farm on August 5, 1930, near Wapakoneta, Ohio. Neil's parents, Stephen and Viola, had two other children—a daughter named June and a son named Dean. Stephen Armstrong worked for the state of Ohio. His job forced the Armstrongs to move around within the state often when Neil was a child.

Neil became interested in flying when he was very young. At just 2 years old, his father took him to the National Air Races in Cleveland, Ohio. *"I must have been a **staunch** aviation fan before I was even **conscious** of it,"* Armstrong

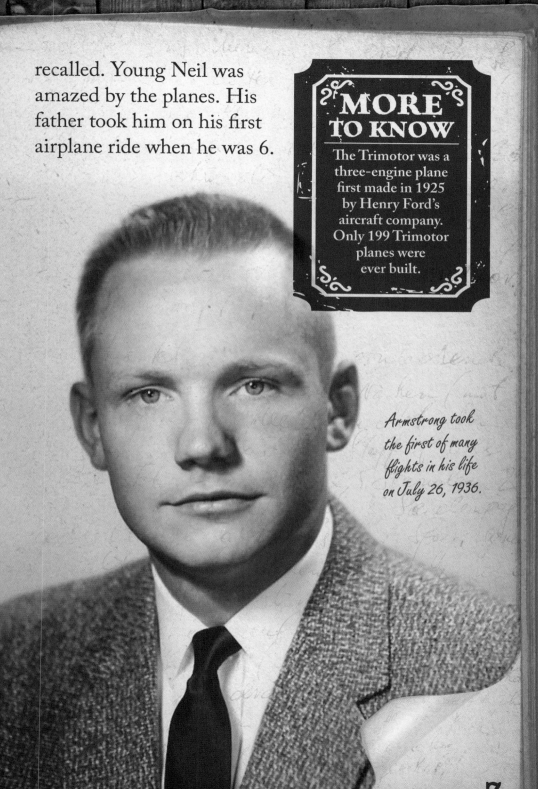

recalled. Young Neil was amazed by the planes. His father took him on his first airplane ride when he was 6.

Armstrong took the first of many flights in his life on July 26, 1936.

Armstrong continued to be impressed by flight throughout his childhood. *"By the time I was nine, I was building model airplanes,"* he said. *"They had become, I suppose, almost an **obsession** with me."* He built a homemade wind tunnel in his basement, which he used to conduct experiments with his model planes. He read books and magazines on flying and airplanes, too.

When Armstrong was 15, he began taking flying lessons. He worked jobs at the airport and around his hometown to pay for the lessons, which taught him to fly an Aeronca Champion plane. Lessons were $9 an hour in 1945—more than $100 in today's money. Armstrong got his pilot's license when he was 16. He could legally fly planes through the air before he could drive cars on the ground!

PURDUE AND KOREA

Armstrong graduated from Blume High School in Wapakoneta in 1947. He joined the US Navy and got a scholarship to attend college. He went to Purdue University to study aeronautical engineering. In 1949, the navy called him to active service. He was stationed aboard the USS *Essex* aircraft carrier and flew 78 combat missions during the Korean War (1950–1953). Armstrong went back to Purdue in 1952 and graduated with a degree in aeronautical engineering.

MORE TO KNOW

Armstrong later got his master's degree in aerospace engineering from the University of Southern California in 1970. He also received a number of honorary degrees from different universities after the Apollo missions.

Neil Armstrong
BS Aeronautical Engineering 1955
Honorary Doctorate 1970

Armstrong received three medals for his service in the US Navy during the Korean War. On one mission, he had to use a **parachute** *to escape a damaged plane.*

The TEST PILOT

In 1955, Armstrong began working as an engineer and test pilot for NACA (National Advisory Committee for Aeronautics) at the Lewis Flight **Propulsion** Laboratories in Cleveland, Ohio. He was soon transferred to the NACA High Speed Flight Station at Edwards Air Force Base in California. Armstrong said the program helped him as an astronaut later in his life. *"Our principal responsibility was*

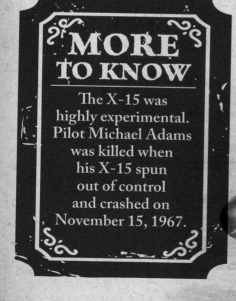

MORE TO KNOW

The X-15 was highly experimental. Pilot Michael Adams was killed when his X-15 spun out of control and crashed on November 15, 1967.

engineering work. We did not do a lot of flying," Armstrong wrote in 1970. *"It was program development, looking at the problems of flight. It was a wonderful time period, and it was very satisfying work, particularly when you found a solution."*

But Armstrong did fly a number of superfast test planes in the late 1950s and early 1960s, including the X-1B and the X-15 rocket plane.

THE X-15

The X-15 rocket plane was a hypersonic research jet. That means it could go five times the speed of sound. Three rocket-powered X-15 jets flew 199 times between 1959 and 1968. The X-15 was attached to a B-52 bomber, then released in the air at a height of 45,000 feet (13,716 m) at around 500 miles (805 km) per hour. Armstrong flew the X-15 seven times, once covering 350 miles (563 km) in about 12 minutes!

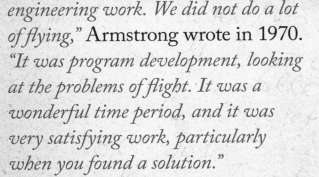

Being a test pilot at Edwards Air Force Base was a dangerous job. In 1952, 62 test pilots died in a 9-month period—almost seven a month.

GOING TO *Space*

The Space Age began in 1957, when the Soviet Union launched *Sputnik I* into orbit around Earth. The beach ball-sized *Sputnik* was the world's first artificial **satellite**. In 1958, NASA was formed with the passage of the National Aeronautics and Space Act. NASA hurried to make the United States first in manned space flight. It picked seven test pilots in 1959 to be the first astronauts. However, when Soviet astronaut, or cosmonaut, Yuri Gagarin went into orbit in 1961, the United States realized it was behind in the "Space Race."

Neil Armstrong was one of nine astronauts NASA selected in its second class in 1962. That same year, President John F. Kennedy gave a stirring speech in which he declared the United States would land a man on the moon by the end of the decade.

Kennedy's "We choose to go to the moon" speech is one of the most famous of his presidency. It set the course for NASA's research and funding for the next decade.

MORE TO KNOW

Early NASA astronauts were test pilots who had experience flying dangerous missions. Today's astronauts are often scientists who do experiments in space.

GEMINI 8

NASA's Gemini program is often called the "bridge to the moon." The space program's focus was testing new ships and equipment for a lunar, or moon, mission and to see if people could live up to 2 weeks in space. The first manned mission, *Gemini 3*, took place in 1965. Each mission was designed to build on what NASA scientists and astronauts learned on previous missions, slowly figuring out how to get to the moon and back.

MORE TO KNOW

Astronauts learned how to spacewalk and to reenter Earth's atmosphere on Gemini missions. NASA also studied the effects of space on the human body, something they're still studying today aboard the International Space Station.

Armstrong was picked as the command pilot for *Gemini 8*, along with pilot Dave Scott. The two were to leave Earth's atmosphere and dock with an unmanned craft called *Agena*. A spacewalk was also planned for the mission, which launched on March 16, 1966.

All Gemini missions, including *Gemini 8*, were launched from a pad called Complex 19 at Cape Canaveral Air Force Station in Florida.

GEMINI AND TITAN

The *Gemini 8* spacecraft was launched on top of a giant rocket, called a Titan II, which created enough thrust to escape Earth's gravitational pull. The Titan had two parts, called stages. Each had its own engine. When the rocket's fuel was spent, the Titan II fell away from the rest of the craft as it entered space. Armstrong thought the ride was smooth. *"The second stage is a real good machine,"* he said a few minutes into the flight.

Once *Gemini 8* reached space, Armstrong got his first view of Earth. *"That's fantastic!"* he exclaimed. The crew then got to work docking. Over 6 hours, they made nine **maneuvers** to dock with *Agena*. It was the first time two ships had docked in space.

Armstrong was thrilled. *"That's just unbelievable!"* he said as they moved within 900 feet (274 m) of *Agena*. *"Unbelievable! I can't believe it!"*

Scott congratulated Armstrong on the docking: *"Outstanding job, Coach!"* But Armstrong was quick to point out that both astronauts had worked hard to make it happen. *"It takes two to tango,"* he said.

However, soon after docking with *Agena*, a stuck thruster sent the two crafts tumbling out of control. Armstrong had to act quickly to save the mission—and their lives.

EMERGENCY LANDING

Spinning about once per second, Armstrong quickly disengaged from *Agena* and tried to control his ship. Using the thrusters meant for reentry into Earth's atmosphere, Armstrong stopped the craft's spin. The move used 75 percent of *Gemini 8*'s reentry fuel, so he had to cut the mission short and head back to Earth. The craft splashed safely into the Pacific Ocean to complete the mission.

MORE TO KNOW

In an airplane or ship, motion from front to back is called roll. Pitch is motion from side to side, and yaw is motion along a vertical, or up and down, axis. *Gemini 8* experienced all three after docking.

Armstrong and Scott are pictured here in *Gemini 8*, along with rescue crew.

To THE MOON

The Apollo program was NASA's attempt to finally land men on the moon, fulfilling the promise in Kennedy's 1961 speech. After the success of the *Gemini 8* mission, Armstrong trained the next 2 years with the Apollo program. He was a backup commander of *Apollo 8*, which sent the first craft to orbit the moon in December 1968.

Six months later, the *Apollo 10* mission came within 50,000 feet (15,240 m) of the moon's surface. The mission was called the "dress rehearsal" for a moon landing, the final test. Armstrong was selected as commander of the mission. Michael Collins was picked as command module pilot, and Edwin "Buzz" Aldrin rounded out the crew as lunar module pilot.

ANOTHER TEST CRASH

While training for *Apollo 11* in 1968, Armstrong crashed a lunar landing research vehicle (LLRV) while testing it at Ellington Air Force Base near Houston, Texas. Though he had flown more than 20 missions in the LLRV, this time the vehicle tilted sharply about 200 feet (61 m) above ground, and he was forced to eject from the pilot's seat. *"I got up and walked away after I landed,"* Armstrong later said. *"The only damage to me was that I bit my tongue."*

PRIME CREW OF FIFTH MANNED APOLLO MISSION

NEIL A. ARMSTRONG   MICHAEL COLLINS   EDWIN E. ALDRIN, JR.

MORE TO KNOW

Astronaut Alan Bean remembered Armstrong went back to his office after the crash: *"I can't think of another person, let alone another astronaut, who would have just gone back to his office after ejecting a fraction of a second before getting killed."*

← *Astronauts often trained in the difficult conditions of deserts to test their endurance.*

APOLLO 11

A 50-50 CHANCE

Of all the aspects of the mission, Armstrong was most worried about the landing. He thought there was a 50 percent chance that they wouldn't be able to pull it off. He and Aldrin had just 12 minutes to bring the *Eagle* from 50,000 feet (15 km) above the moon to the surface safely—even though the craft would be traveling thousands of miles per hour. There was only enough fuel for one landing attempt.

The *Apollo 11* crew lifted off from Kennedy Space Center in Florida on July 16, 1969. A three-stage Saturn V rocket drove the spacecraft out of Earth's atmosphere. It entered Earth's orbit about 12 minutes after launch. Then, the rocket's third stage fired up to head the craft toward the moon at a speed of 24,200 miles (38,946 km) per hour. After the last stage of the Saturn V rocket detached, the remaining parts of the spacecraft were the command and service module, called *Columbia*, and the lunar module, called *Eagle*. They entered the moon's orbit on July 19.

On July 20, Armstrong and Buzz Aldrin separated *Eagle* from *Columbia* and prepared to land. *"Man, this is really something; you ought to look at this,"* Armstrong said, amazed at the moon's craters and mountains.

Command
Module

Service
Module

Lunar
Module

MORE TO KNOW

The lunar module began its descent to the moon after its 13th orbit.

Apollo 11 blasted off from Launch Pad 39A as a large crowd watched a few miles away.

21

"THE EAGLE" Has Landed

MORE TO KNOW

The *Eagle* landed with about 20 seconds of fuel remaining!

Unfortunately, as the *Eagle* made its descent, the astronauts lost communication with the mission control center in Houston, Texas. Alarms told them the computer was overloading—and it was in control of the *Eagle*'s speed and positioning. Though mission control corrected the problems, Armstrong missed spotting the landmarks he had planned to use to find a landing area. The computer was set to land them in a crater!

Armstrong took over piloting and found a flat surface. Despite blowing moon dust making the descent more difficult, he brought down the module gently and said the famous words: *"Houston, Tranquility Base here. The Eagle has landed."*

Armstrong was thrilled: *"That, in my view, was . . . the emotional high. And the business of getting down the ladder to me was much less significant."*

The area of the moon where the *Eagle* was brought down was called Mare Tranquillitatis, or the Sea of Tranquility. It was a smooth and level area.

PREPARED
FOR THE WORST

Armstrong and Aldrin knew there was a chance they would never leave the moon's surface. Even US president Richard Nixon had a speech ready in case something went wrong. The speech began: *"Fate has **ordained** that the men who went to the moon to explore in peace will stay on the moon to rest in peace. These brave men, Neil Armstrong and Edwin Aldrin, know that there is no hope for their recovery. But they also know that there is hope for mankind in their sacrifice."* Thankfully, Nixon didn't have to use it!

SMALL *Steps*

Four hours after landing, Neil Armstrong left the lunar module, set up a TV camera, and got ready to take his first steps on the moon. About 110 hours into the mission, Neil Armstrong became the first man to walk on the moon.

The 600 million people watching on Earth heard Armstrong say his most famous words: *"That's one small step for man, one giant leap for mankind."* Aldrin followed Armstrong about 20 minutes later. He called the rocky satellite's surface *"magnificent* **desolation**."

The matter that covers the moon's surface, mostly a gray soil, is called lunar regolith. Armstrong described it: *"The surface is fine and powdery. I can kick it up loosely with my toe. It does adhere in fine layers, like powdered charcoal, to the sole and sides of my boots."*

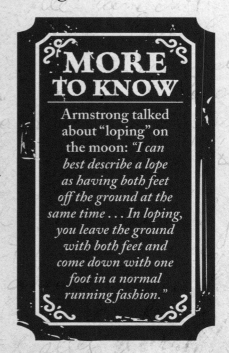

MORE TO KNOW

Armstrong talked about "loping" on the moon: *"I can best describe a lope as having both feet off the ground at the same time . . . In loping, you leave the ground with both feet and come down with one foot in a normal running fashion."*

THE FAMOUS QUOTE

Some think Armstrong actually said, *"That's one small step for a man . . ."* They believe the "a" wasn't picked up by the transmission equipment. Armstrong later confirmed that. Armstrong's brother Dean said the quote wasn't made up on the spot. He said, before the mission, Armstrong had asked for his opinion about it. However, others say Neil told them he thought of it just as he was preparing for that famous step.

Moon dust got everywhere. It covered spacesuits, tools, and other objects that came back to Earth from the mission.

On the SURFACE

COLUMBIA RETURNS

The lunar module lifted off the moon's surface on July 21 and docked with the command module. Then, *Columbia*, with all three astronauts in it, began the return trip to Earth. The lunar module was left in the moon's orbit and later crashed to the surface. The crew had few problems on their return from the moon. *Columbia* splashed down in the Pacific Ocean on July 24, 1969, completing the 8-day mission and returning the heroes to their home planet.

Armstrong spent about 2 1/2 hours walking on the moon's surface. He and Aldrin performed scientific experiments, collected almost 50 pounds (23 kg) of surface samples, and took photos. They also planted an American flag on the moon. They traveled about 3,300 feet (1 km) during their moonwalk, but there wasn't enough time to explore everything.

"There were a lot of interesting areas within 500 feet or so to go and look at if we had had the time," Armstrong said. *"It would have been interesting to take that time and go out and inspect them closely and get some pictures, but that was a luxury we didn't have."*

MORE TO KNOW

Armstrong and Aldrin were awake 22 hours straight when they went back inside the lunar module. The astronauts were supposed to get some sleep before leaving the surface, but they had trouble getting comfortable in the extreme cold.

The three *Apollo 11* astronauts were placed in **quarantine** until August 10. They were tested for illnesses and other conditions.

HORNET + 3

AFTER
the Moon

The Apollo astronauts were honored with a parade in New York City when they returned to Earth. They then went on a world tour so people of other countries could celebrate them as heroes. A reporter asked Neil Armstrong how he would live a normal life after landing on the moon. He thought for a moment, smiled, and said, *"It kind of depends on you."*

Armstrong would never return to space, but he did live as quiet a life as he wished. He worked at NASA until 1971. He went on to teach engineering at the University of Cincinnati until 1979. He then worked for various companies and government agencies. He was even a voice for a character in a NASA cartoon film in 2010. Neil Armstrong died in his home state of Ohio in 2012.

Armstrong's actual signature:

TIMELINE
THE LIFE OF NEIL ARMSTRONG

1930 — Neil Alden Armstrong is born on August 5 near Wapakoneta, Ohio.

1936 — Armstrong takes his first flight, in a Ford Trimotor plane.

1946 — Armstrong receives his pilot's license.

1947 — Armstrong begins to attend Purdue University.

1949 — The US Navy calls Armstrong to active service during the Korean War. He flies 78 combat missions.

1952 — Armstrong graduates from Purdue with a degree in aeronautical engineering.

1955 — Armstrong begins working as a test pilot for the National Advisory Committee for Aeronautics.

1962 — Armstrong is chosen to be a NASA astronaut.

1966 — *Gemini 8*, with Armstrong as command pilot, launches into space.

1969 — *Apollo 11* launches with Armstrong as mission commander. Armstrong walks on the moon on July 20.

1971 — Armstrong resigns from NASA and begins to teach at the University of Cincinnati.

1985 — Armstrong serves on the National Commission on Space.

2012 — Armstrong dies on August 25 in Cincinnati, Ohio.

FIGHTING FOR NASA

Armstrong's rare moments in the public spotlight after *Apollo 11* came when he spoke in Washington, DC, about funding for NASA. *"I was glad to have the experience, although I think everybody should have to go to Washington and spend a little time—just to see how difficult it is to run this country,"* a frustrated Armstrong said to NASA historians in a 2001 interview. *"It's really hard to get things done there."*

GLOSSARY

conscious: aware of something

desolation: barren wasteland

finite: having limits

ledger: a book that a company uses to record information about the money it has paid and received

maneuver: a planned movement

module: a part of a space vehicle that can work alone

obsession: someone or something that a person thinks about constantly or frequently

ordain: to issue an order

parachute: a piece of equipment made of cloth that is fastened to someone that allows them to fall slowly and land safely after they have jumped or been dropped from an aircraft

propulsion: the force that moves something forward

quarantine: the keeping of someone or something away from the public to stop the spread of disease

satellite: an object that moves around a larger body in space

staunch: very devoted or loyal

FOR MORE
Information

Books

Hubbard, Ben. *Neil Armstrong and Getting to the Moon*. Chicago, IL: Heinemann Raintree, 2016.

Yomtov, Nelson. *Neil Armstrong Walks on the Moon*. Minneapolis, MN: Bellwether Media. 2016.

Websites

Apollo 11
airandspace.si.edu/explore-and-learn/topics/apollo/apollo-program/landing-missions/apollo11.cfm
See photos and learn more facts about *Apollo 11* on this Smithsonian site.

Apollo 11 Landing
nasa.gov/externalflash/apollo11_landing
Learn more about the *Apollo 11* landing site with this interactive NASA website.

We Choose the Moon
wechoosethemoon.org
Follow the *Apollo 11* mission with this minute-by-minute recreation.

INDEX